delicious.

Bake

Welcome

I get more requests for cake recipes than any other type of dish so I know I am not alone in my passion for baking.

In *Bake* I have compiled some of my favourite treats – from individual cakes and pastries for special occasions, to pies and tarts for when you need something warm, and luscious desserts for entertaining at home. All the recipes are easy to follow so whether you are a casual cook or a committed baker there is sure to be something you will love.

When friends drop by, there is nothing better than having a batch of scones or a cake fresh from the oven to offer around. So don't delay: turn on the oven, pop on your apron, let's have fun in the kitchen and bake!

Valli

Contents

Cakes

Cupcakes, muffins and cookies

Tarts and pies

Savoury tarts and pies

Puddings and desserts

Red wine chocolate cake

1⅓ cups (200g) plain flour

2 tbs Dutch cocoa, plus extra
to dust

1 tsp baking powder

½ tsp bicarbonate of soda

225g softened unsalted
butter

1 cup (220g) caster sugar

4 eggs

200g dark chocolate, melted,
cooled

1 tsp vanilla extract

½ cup (125ml) milk

½ cup (125ml) red wine

Fresh raspberries and
whipped cream, to serve

Ganache

150g dark chocolate,
chopped

½ cup (125ml) pure (thin)
cream

20g unsalted butter

Preheat the oven to 160°C. Grease a 2.4L bundt pan.

Sift together flour, cocoa, baking powder and bicarbonate of soda onto a sheet of baking paper.

Using an electric mixer, beat the butter and sugar for 3–4 minutes until thick and pale. Add eggs 1 at a time, beating well after each addition. Gently fold in melted chocolate until combined. Beating gently, slowly add flour mixture until combined, then add vanilla, milk and red wine, and beat to combine. Spoon batter into prepared pan, levelling the top with the back of the spoon.

Bake for 45–50 minutes until a skewer comes out clean when inserted into the cake. Cool cake in pan for 10 minutes before turning out onto a wire rack to cool completely.

Meanwhile, to make ganache, place all ingredients in a bowl set over a saucepan of gently simmering water (don't let the bowl touch the water) for 3–4 minutes until chocolate melts. Remove bowl from pan, stir until well combined, then allow to cool at room temperature.

To serve, dust cake with extra cocoa, then drizzle over the ganache and serve with raspberries and whipped cream. **Serves 8**

Chocolate mayonnaise cake

1⅔ cups (250g) self-raising
　　flour
60g cocoa powder
¼ tsp baking powder
200g caster sugar
¾ cup (225g) whole-egg
　　mayonnaise
3 tsp vanilla extract
100g unsalted butter,
　　softened
100g cream cheese
1⅔ cups (250g) pure icing
　　sugar, sifted
1 shot (30ml) Kahlua (or other
　　coffee liqueur)
Hazelnuts half-dipped
　　in melted chocolate,
　　to decorate

Preheat the oven to 180°C. Grease and line the base of a 23cm springform cake pan.

Place the flour, cocoa, baking powder, caster sugar, mayonnaise and 2 teaspoons of the vanilla in the bowl of an electric mixer with 200ml warm water and beat for 2–3 minutes until smooth. Spread into the prepared pan and bake for 40 minutes or until a skewer inserted in the centre comes out clean. Cool completely.

Meanwhile, make the icing. Process the butter, cream cheese, icing sugar, remaining 1 teaspoon of vanilla and Kahlua in a food processor until smooth. Spread over the cooled cake and decorate with nuts. **Serves 6–8**

Chocolate cheesecake with cocoa nib cream

2 x 150g packets Oreo
    biscuits or other cream-
    filled chocolate biscuits
125g unsalted butter,
    melted, cooled
250g cream cheese,
    at room temperature
2 cups (500g) mascarpone
⅓ cup (75g) caster sugar
3 eggs
½ cup (50g) cocoa powder
100g dark chocolate,
    melted, cooled
1 tbs chocolate liqueur
    (optional)
1 cup (120g) cocoa nibs
    (roast cocoa bean pieces)*,
    plus extra to serve
300ml thickened cream,
    lightly whipped

Grease and line a 24cm springform cake pan with baking paper.

Place the biscuits in a food processor and whiz to fine crumbs. Add the butter and pulse a few times to combine, then press into the base of the cake pan. Chill for 30 minutes to firm up.

Preheat the oven to 170°C.

Place the cream cheese, mascarpone and caster sugar in the cleaned food processor and whiz to combine. Add the eggs and whiz to combine, then add the cocoa, chocolate and liqueur, if using, and whiz until very smooth. Add half the cocoa nibs and pulse to combine, then spread the mascarpone mixture over the biscuit base.

Bake for 45–50 minutes until the cake is firm to the touch, but still has a slight wobble. Turn off the oven and allow the cheesecake to cool completely in the oven with the door slightly ajar. Once cooled, chill for 2–3 hours until firm.

Fold the remaining ½ cup (60g) cocoa nibs into the whipped cream. Top the cheesecake with the cocoa nib cream and serve sprinkled with extra cocoa nibs. **Serves 8**

* Cocoa nibs are available from gourmet food shops and specialist chocolate shops.

Passioncake

Pulp from 8 passionfruits
(to give about 200ml
passionfruit pulp)
100g desiccated coconut
¾ cup (165g) caster sugar
½ cup (75g) plain flour, sifted
4 eggs, lightly beaten
125g unsalted butter, melted
1 tsp lemon juice
Raspberries, to serve

Passionfruit icing
50g unsalted butter, softened
3 cups (450g) icing sugar,
sifted
Pulp from 3 passionfruits
(to give about ¼ cup
passionfruit pulp)

Preheat the oven to 180°C. Grease and line an 18cm x 16cm heart-shaped cake pan or 18cm round springform cake pan.

Place the passionfruit pulp in a food processor and pulse several times to loosen the pulp from the seeds. Set aside.

Combine coconut, sugar and flour in a bowl. Fold in the eggs, butter, lemon juice and passionfruit pulp and seeds until combined. Pour into the cake pan and bake for 35–40 minutes until a skewer inserted into the centre comes out clean. Cool in the pan for 5 minutes, then turn out onto a wire rack to cool completely.

For the passionfruit icing, place the butter and icing sugar in an electric mixer. Beat until doubled in size, then add the passionfruit pulp, mixing well until combined.

Spread the icing over the cooled cake, then decorate with the raspberries and serve. **Serves 4**

Orange-lavender syrup cake

250g unsalted butter,
  softened
1 cup (220g) caster sugar
4 eggs
⅓ cup (50g) plain flour, sifted
2 tsp baking powder
Finely grated zest and juice
  of 2 oranges
250g fine semolina
2 cups (250g) almond meal
120g thick Greek-style
  yoghurt
250g punnet strawberries,
  halved or quartered

Syrup

Finely grated zest and juice
  of 2 oranges
1 tbs dried lavender flowers*
2 cinnamon quills
1¼ cups (275g) caster sugar

Preheat the oven to 170°C. Grease a 23cm round springform pan, line the base with baking paper and lightly dust the sides with flour, shaking off any excess.

Beat the butter and sugar in an electric mixer until thick and pale. Add the eggs, one at a time, beating well after each addition. Fold in the flour and baking powder, followed by the orange zest, semolina and almond meal. Add orange juice and yoghurt and gently stir until combined. Pour into the prepared pan and bake for 1 hour or until a skewer inserted into the centre comes out clean. Cool in the pan for 5 minutes.

Meanwhile, for the syrup, place all the ingredients in a saucepan with 1½ cups (375ml) water. Stir over low heat to dissolve the sugar, then simmer for 20–25 minutes until slightly thickened.

Prick the surface of the warm cake all over with a skewer. Slowly drizzle over half the syrup, then allow to cool.

Toss the strawberries in the remaining syrup, then drizzle over the cake and serve. **Serves 6–8**

* Dried lavender flowers are available from selected delis and Herbie's Spices: herbies.com.au

Red wine pear & almond cake

1½ cups (375ml) red wine

300g caster sugar

2 cinnamon quills

3 firm pears (such as beurre
    bosc), peeled, cored, cut
    into thin wedges

150g unsalted butter

3 eggs

½ cup (75g) plain flour, sifted

150g almond meal

1½ tsp baking powder

Place the red wine and 150g sugar in a saucepan over low heat, stirring until the sugar dissolves. Add the cinnamon and pears, then cover the surface closely with a piece of baking paper cut to fit (cartouche) and cook for 10 minutes or until the pears are tender. Set aside to cool completely in the poaching liquid.

Preheat the oven to 180°C and grease a 22cm springform cake pan.

Beat the butter and remaining 150g sugar with electric beaters until thick and pale. Add the eggs, 1 at a time, beating well after each addition. Fold in the flour, almond meal and baking powder. Set aside.

Drain the pears, reserving the poaching liquid. Arrange the pear slices in the cake pan in a circular pattern, slightly overlapping. Spread over the cake batter, smoothing the top with a spatula. Bake for 35–40 minutes until a skewer inserted into the centre comes out clean. Cool in the pan for 10 minutes.

Meanwhile, place the pear poaching liquid in a saucepan over medium-high heat and cook for 6–8 minutes until reduced and syrupy.

Invert cake onto a serving plate. Brush the warm cake with the poaching syrup. Serve warm or cool. **Serves 6–8**

Black forest cake

680g jar pitted morello
    cherries*, drained, juice
    reserved
2 tbs sugar
⅓ cup (80ml) kirsch* or
    brandy
2 tsp arrowroot
2 tbs pure icing sugar, sifted
300g mascarpone
350g store-bought chocolate
    slab cake or chocolate
    brownies
2 tbs cherry jam
1 tbs finely grated dark
    chocolate, to garnish
Zest of 1 orange, to garnish

Place the cherry juice in a saucepan over low heat with the sugar and half the kirsch or brandy. Mix the arrowroot with a little cold water until smooth, then add to the pan. Heat gently, stirring, for 2–3 minutes until thickened. Add the cherries to the sauce, then remove from the heat and set aside to cool.

Beat the icing sugar and mascarpone together in a bowl with a wooden spoon until combined.

Cut the cake into 6 pieces and place on a platter. Sprinkle over remaining kirsch and spread with the jam. Pile the mascarpone mixture on top of the cake pieces followed by some cherries and sauce. Sprinkle with chocolate and zest, then serve with remaining cherry sauce. **Serves 6**

* Morello cherries are available from supermarkets. Kirsch is a clear, unsweetened cherry brandy, available from bottle shops.

Pistachio cake with sugar-coated rose petals

250g unsalted butter, softened

1 cup (220g) caster sugar

½ tsp vanilla extract

Finely grated zest of 1 lemon, plus 1 tbs lemon juice

4 eggs

⅓ cup (50g) plain flour

100g almond meal

⅔ cup (100g) pistachio kernels, ground

1 tsp baking powder

1⅔ cups (250g) icing sugar, sifted

Sugar-coated rose petals

4–6 unsprayed fresh rose petals

1 eggwhite, whisked until frothy

⅓ cup (75g) caster sugar

Preheat the oven to 180°C. Grease and line a 23cm springform cake pan with baking paper.

Place the butter, caster sugar, vanilla and lemon zest in a large bowl and beat with electric beaters until thick and pale. Add the eggs, 1 at a time, beating well after each addition, then fold in the flour, almond meal, ground pistachio, baking powder and a good pinch of salt. Spread into the cake pan.

Bake for 40 minutes or until a skewer inserted into the centre comes out clean. Cool the cake in the pan for 10 minutes, then transfer to a wire rack to cool completely.

Meanwhile, for the sugar-coated rose petals, use a pastry brush to lightly coat the rose petals with the eggwhite, then sprinkle with caster sugar, shaking off any excess. Place on a wire rack and stand at room temperature for 1 hour or until crisp and dry.

Place icing sugar and lemon juice in a bowl. Stir in 2 tablespoons warm water until you have a soft dropping consistency, adding more water if necessary.

Pour the icing over the cooled cake, allowing some to drip down the sides. Serve garnished with the sugar-coated rose petals.

Serves 6–8

Yoghurt cake with sangria-poached fruit

1 cup (280g) thick
   Greek-style yoghurt,
   plus extra to serve
1 cup (220g) caster sugar
1 tsp vanilla extract
⅓ cup (80ml) sunflower oil
2 eggs
1⅔ cups (250g) plain flour
1½ tsp baking powder
1 tsp bicarbonate of soda
Finely grated zest of 1 lemon
Finely grated zest of 1 orange
Icing sugar, to dust

Sangria-poached fruit
3 cups (750ml) red wine
400g frozen mixed berries
½ cup (110g) caster sugar
1 vanilla bean, split,
   seeds scraped
Pared rind of ½ lemon
Pared rind of ½ orange
2 dark plums, halved, stoned
2 pears, cored, quartered
4 figs, halved
1 cup (150g) cherries

Preheat the oven to 170°C. Grease and line the base and sides of a 20cm round springform cake pan with baking paper.

Combine yoghurt, caster sugar and vanilla in a bowl and whisk until smooth. Whisk in the oil until well combined, then add the eggs, one at a time, beating well with a wooden spoon after each addition. Sift the flour, baking powder and bicarbonate of soda into the bowl, then add the citrus zest and a pinch of salt and stir to combine.

Spread the cake batter into the prepared pan and bake for 45 minutes or until a skewer inserted in the centre comes out clean. (Cover loosely with foil if the cake is browning too quickly.) Allow to cool completely in the pan, then dust with icing sugar.

Meanwhile, for the sangria-poached fruit, place the wine, mixed berries and sugar in a saucepan over low heat, stirring to dissolve sugar. Bring to a simmer and cook for 10 minutes or until the berries are soft. Remove from the heat and stand for 30 minutes to allow flavours to infuse. Pass through a fine sieve, pressing down on the solids to extract the juices. Discard the solids, then return the liquid to the pan. Add vanilla pod and seeds and pared citrus rind to the liquid, then add the plums, pears, figs and cherries. Place over medium-low heat and bring to a simmer. Cook for 8 minutes or until the fruit is tender (the cooking time will vary depending on the ripeness of the pears). Serve the sangria-poached fruit warm or chilled with the yoghurt cake and extra yoghurt. **Serves 6–8**

Crumbly olive oil, rosemary & pear cake

1½ cups (225g) plain flour

¾ cup (120g) wholemeal
or spelt flour

¾ cup (165g) caster sugar

1½ tsp baking powder

3 eggs

1¼ cups (310ml) fruity
extra virgin olive oil

1 tsp vanilla extract

4 small pears, peeled, cored,
cut into 1cm pieces, to give
2 cups

2 tsp chopped rosemary
leaves

¼ cup (35g) currants

Mascarpone, to serve

Preheat the oven to 180°C.

Grease a 26cm, 3cm-deep loose-bottomed tart pan.

Sift flours together into a bowl. Add sugar and baking powder. Beat eggs, olive oil and vanilla, then add to flour mixture, stirring to combine. Gently fold through pear, rosemary and currants (with any soaking liquid, if using). Spoon batter into tart pan, then bake for 55 minutes or until cake is golden and a skewer comes out clean when inserted into centre. Cool in pan for 10 minutes, then transfer to a wire rack to cool completely. Serve warm or at room temperature with mascarpone. **Serves 6–8**

Scandi cake

250g softened unsalted
  butter
1 cup (220g) caster sugar
3 eggs
1½ cups (225g) self-raising
  flour
⅔ cup (100g) plain flour
¼ cup (60ml) milk
1½ tbs lemon juice

Toppings

Dulce de leche*
Lemon curd*
Raspberry sauce*
Fresh fruit
Chopped nuts
Thick cream

Preheat the oven to 170°C. Grease a 10cm x 21cm loaf pan and line base and sides with baking paper.

Beat butter and sugar with electric beaters for 3–4 minutes until thick and pale. Add eggs 1 at a time, beating well after each addition. Sift in flours, then stir through milk and lemon juice.

Spoon batter into the pan, then bake for 1 hour (cover loosely with foil if browning too quickly) or until a skewer inserted into the centre comes out clean.

Cool cake in the pan for 10 minutes, then transfer to a wire rack to cool completely. To serve, thickly slice cake and serve with your choice of toppings, fruit, nuts and thick cream. **Serves 6–8**

* Dulce de leche is a South American milk caramel, available in jars from selected delis, supermarkets and gourmet food shops; or see recipe, p 38. Lemon curd and raspberry sauce are available from delis and gourmet food shops.

Peanut butter cheesecake

400g digestive biscuits

50g ground almonds

120g unsalted butter, melted, cooled

350g fresh ricotta, drained

500g cream cheese

1 cup firmly packed (250g) brown sugar

4 eggs

1 cup (280g) peanut butter (crunchy or smooth)

1 tsp vanilla extract

300ml pure (thin) cream

300ml sour cream

200ml thickened cream

12 peanut butter chocolates* (optional)

Grease a 23cm springform cake pan.

Combine biscuits and almond meal in a food processor and pulse to the consistency of coarse breadcrumbs. Add butter and pulse until mixture just comes together. Press mixture into the base of the cake pan, then refrigerate for 30 minutes.

Preheat the oven to 160°C.

Place ricotta, cream cheese and brown sugar in the bowl of an electric mixer and beat for 1–2 minutes until smooth. Add eggs 1 at a time, beating well after each addition. Add peanut butter, vanilla, pure (thin) cream and sour cream, then beat on low speed until mixture is smooth and combined.

Spread ricotta mixture over the biscuit base, then wrap the outside base and side of the cake pan with a double sheet of aluminium foil, ensuring there are no gaps. Place pan in a deep baking pan, then pour in enough water to come halfway up the side. Bake for 1½ hours or until cheesecake is almost set, but the centre still has a slight wobble. Turn off the oven and set the oven door ajar with a wooden spoon. Leave cheesecake to cool in the oven for 1 hour, then remove and refrigerate for 3 hours.

Whip thickened cream to soft peaks, then spread over the top of the cheesecake. Break chocolates into chunks, if using, and scatter over the top. Serve with a health warning! **Serves 8–10**

* We used Hershey's Reese's peanut butter cups, available from Thomas Dux, selected confectioners and gourmet food shops.

Panettone cake

1½ cups (250g) sultanas
¼ cup (60ml) Marsala*
   or brandy
600g panettone* or brioche
   loaf, thickly sliced
80g softened unsalted butter
⅔ cup (100g) dried
   cranberries
8 eggs
600ml thickened cream
1 cup (250ml) milk
⅔ cup (150g) caster sugar
1 tsp vanilla extract
Icing sugar and pure (thin)
   cream, to serve

Place sultanas and Marsala in a small bowl and set aside to soak for 30 minutes.

Grease a 24cm springform cake pan. Place a double piece of paper towel on a baking tray and set the pan on top (some egg mixture will seep through the bottom of the cake pan, so the paper will absorb it).

Spread each slice of panettone with butter, then layer slices in the pan, scattering sultana mixture and cranberries over each layer.

Whisk together eggs, cream, milk, caster sugar and vanilla until combined. Pour egg mixture over the layered panettone, then set aside for 30 minutes for the egg mixture to soak in.

Preheat the oven to 150°C. Remove paper towel from baking tray, then transfer tray with cake pan to the oven and bake for 1¼ hours or until just set. Rest for 15 minutes in the pan before turning out.

Dust with icing sugar and serve with cream. **Serves 6–8**

* Marsala is a Sicilian fortified wine, available from bottle shops. Panettone is available from gourmet food shops and delis.

Banana fruit loaf

1 cup (160g) sultanas

¾ cup (125g) raisins

125g currants

1 cup (250ml) cold, black tea

2 tbs brandy (optional)

2 ripe bananas, mashed

1 cup firmly packed (220g)
   brown sugar

1 cup (100g) chopped
   walnuts

¼ cup (50g) glace cherries,
   halved

1 egg, lightly beaten

2 tbs milk

2 tbs treacle

2⅔ cups (400g) self-raising
   flour, sifted

Butter, to serve

Place the sultanas, raisins and currants in a large bowl with the tea and brandy. Cover and leave to soak overnight.

The next day, preheat the oven to 180°C. Grease a 1-litre loaf pan and line the base and sides with baking paper.

Add the bananas, brown sugar, walnuts, cherries, egg, milk and treacle to the fruit. Sift in the flour, then fold everything together and spread in the prepared pan. Bake for 1¼ hours or until a skewer inserted in the centre comes out clean. (Cover loosely with foil if browning too quickly.)

Cool the cake in the pan for 10 minutes, then turn out onto a rack to cool completely. Slice and serve with butter, if desired.

Serves 6–8

Carrot cake

1 cup (250ml) sunflower oil
1 cup (220g) caster sugar
3 eggs
1½ cups (225g) self-raising
    flour
1 large carrot, finely grated
Finely grated zest of
    1 orange
¾ cup (75g) toasted walnuts,
    finely chopped

Cream cheese frosting
50g unsalted butter
250g soft cream cheese
2 tbs pure icing sugar, sifted
1 tsp pure vanilla extract

Preheat the oven to 180°C. Grease an 18cm x 25cm lamington pan and line with baking paper, leaving some overhanging the sides.

Place the oil and sugar in a bowl and combine using a hand whisk. Whisk in the eggs, then sift in the flour and fold together to combine. Stir in the grated carrot, orange zest and ½ cup (50g) of the walnuts.

Spread the mixture into the prepared pan and bake for 40 minutes or until a skewer inserted in the centre comes out clean. Cool in the pan for 10 minutes, then use the overhanging paper to remove the cake. Cool completely on a rack.

Meanwhile, for the icing, whiz all the ingredients in a food processor or beat with electric beaters until smooth. Spread over the cooled cake, then sprinkle with the remaining chopped walnuts before slicing. **Serves 6–8**

Sticky date loaf

250g pitted dates
60g unsalted butter,
    roughly chopped
180g caster sugar
2 tbs golden syrup,
    plus extra to serve
1 tsp bicarbonate of soda
2 eggs, lightly beaten
180g plain flour, sifted
1 tsp baking powder
Cream cheese or butter,
    to spread

Preheat the oven to 170°C. Grease a 25cm x 10cm loaf pan and line with baking paper.

Place the dates and 1 cup (250ml) water in a saucepan and bring to the boil, then decrease the heat to low and simmer for 3–4 minutes until all the liquid has absorbed and the dates are mushy. Mash to break up any big pieces, then add the butter, sugar and golden syrup. Stir until the butter has melted, then remove from the heat and stir the bicarbonate of soda into the hot mixture. Cool slightly, then stir in the egg. Fold in the flour and baking powder, then spread the batter into the pan and bake for 30 minutes or until a skewer inserted into the centre comes out clean (cover loosely with foil if browning too quickly).

Cool slightly in the pan, then turn out onto a rack to cool completely. Slice and serve with cream cheese or butter to spread, and golden syrup to drizzle. **Serves 6–8**

Dulce de leche cupcakes

125g unsalted butter,
   softened
½ tsp vanilla extract
¾ cup (165g) caster sugar
3 eggs
2 cups (300g) self-raising flour
¼ cup (60ml) milk

Dulce de leche*
2 x 395g cans sweetened
   condensed milk

To make the dulce de leche, remove and discard labels from milk cans, then make 2 small holes in the top of each with a can opener. Place in a saucepan, opened-side up, and add enough water to almost cover cans. Bring to the boil, then adjust heat to a gentle simmer and cook for 3 hours, topping up with boiling water so it stays at the same level. Using an oven glove, carefully remove cans from water. Cool completely, then open cans and scoop the thick caramel out into a container. (Keeps covered in fridge for up to 2 weeks.)

Preheat the oven to 180°C. Grease a 12-hole muffin pan or line with paper cases.

Using electric beaters, mix the butter, vanilla, sugar, eggs, flour and milk together on medium speed for 3 minutes until smooth and pale. Divide the batter among the muffin holes and bake for 25 minutes or until a skewer inserted into the centre comes out clean.

Cool cupcakes slightly in the pan, then turn out and place on a rack to cool completely. Spread the cooled cakes with dulce de leche. **Makes 12**

* Dulce de leche, a South American milk caramel, is also available in jars from selected delis, supermarkets and gourmet food shops.

Sweet sliders

3 cups (450g) plain flour
1½ tbs caster sugar
3 tsp dried instant yeast
1 egg, lightly beaten
60g softened unsalted butter
1 cup (250ml) milk, heated,
   plus extra to brush
200ml thickened cream
1 tbs sifted icing sugar,
   plus extra to dust
Scraped seeds of 1 vanilla
   bean or 1 tsp vanilla extract
½ cup (160g) strawberry jam
Sliced strawberries, to serve

Combine flour, caster sugar and yeast in a bowl. Add ½ tsp salt and make a well in the centre. Add egg, butter and 1 cup (250ml) warm milk, then stir with a wooden spoon to make a soft dough, adding more milk if necessary. Place in an oiled bowl, cover with a clean tea towel and set aside to prove in a warm place for 1 hour or until doubled in size.

Preheat the oven to 190°C. Grease a 26cm round cake pan.

Turn out dough onto a lightly floured surface and knead for 3 minutes or until smooth and elastic. Divide into 12 portions, then shape each into a ball and place side by side in the pan. Cover with a clean tea towel and set aside to prove in a warm place for a further 20 minutes.

Brush tops with extra milk, then bake for 20–25 minutes or until golden. Remove from pan and transfer to a wire rack to cool.

Meanwhile, whisk the cream, icing sugar and vanilla seeds to soft peaks.

To serve, split each bun in half, spread with strawberry jam, top with cream and sliced strawberries, sandwich halves together and dust with icing sugar. **Makes 12**

Rosewater cupcakes

180g unsalted butter,
  softened
350g caster sugar
4 eggs
1 cup (250ml) milk
1 tsp each vanilla extract and
  rosewater*
1⅓ cups (200g) self-raising
  flour
1 cup (150g) plain flour

Icing

500g unsalted butter,
  softened
350g pure icing sugar, sifted
Rose pink food colouring

Preheat the oven to 180°C and line a 12-hole muffin pan with paper cases.

Place the butter in the bowl of an electric mixer and beat for 5 minutes until very pale. Gradually add the sugar and continue to beat for a further 5 minutes until very light and pale. Add the eggs, one at a time, beating well after each addition.

Combine the milk, vanilla and rosewater in a bowl. Sift the flours and gently fold into the egg mixture using a metal spoon, alternating with the milk mixture, until combined. Spoon into paper cases, filling to just over halfway. Bake for 20 minutes or until a skewer inserted in the centre comes out clean and the cakes are lightly golden. Stand in the pan for 5 minutes, then turn out onto a wire rack to cool completely.

For the icing, beat the butter, icing sugar and a few drops of colouring with electric beaters until light and fluffy. Use a piping bag with a fluted nozzle to ice the cakes generously. **Makes 12**

* Rosewater is available from supermarkets and Middle Eastern food shops.

Triple-chocolate fudge cookies

250g unsalted butter

¾ cup (165g) caster sugar

¾ cup (185g) brown sugar

1 tsp vanilla extract

1 egg

2 cups (300g) plain flour,
  sifted

¼ cup (25g) cocoa, sifted

1 tsp bicarbonate of soda

⅓ cup (40g) chopped
  roasted hazelnuts

100g salted caramel
  chocolate*, chopped

150g dark chocolate,
  chopped

150g white chocolate,
  chopped

Preheat the oven to 180°C.

Line 2 large baking trays with baking paper.

Place the butter, caster sugar, brown sugar and vanilla extract in an electric mixer and beat until thick and pale. Add the egg and beat until well combined. Sift in flour, cocoa and bicarbonate of soda, then stir in hazelnuts, salted caramel chocolate and ⅔ cup (120g) each of the dark and white chocolate. Roll level tablespoons of cookie dough into balls, then arrange on the trays 5cm apart. Slightly flatten each ball with your hand, then bake for 12 minutes or until just dry on the surface. Allow to cool until slightly firm, then transfer to a wire rack to cool completely.

Place the reserved 30g dark chocolate in a heatproof bowl set over a saucepan of simmering water (don't let the bowl touch the water). Stir until melted, then drizzle over the biscuits. Repeat with the remaining 30g white chocolate. Cool until chocolate sets.

Makes 36 large cookies

* We used Mazet milk salted caramel chocolate, available from Simon Johnson, simonjohnson.com.au; substitute regular milk chocolate.

Blueberry & lemon scones with lemon drizzle icing

300ml pure (thin) cream
2 cups (300g) plain flour
1 tsp baking powder
2 tbs caster sugar
100g unsalted butter,
    cut into small pieces
2 tsp finely grated lemon
    zest, plus ½–1 tbs juice
125g punnet blueberries
1 cup (150g) sifted
    icing sugar
Whipped cream and
    lemon curd*

Preheat the oven to 220°C. Grease and flour a baking tray.

Set aside 1 tablespoon pure (thin) cream to brush tops of scones.

Sift flour and baking powder into a bowl. Add sugar and ½ teaspoon salt, then rub the butter into the flour mixture until the consistency of fine breadcrumbs. Add lemon zest, blueberries and remaining pure (thin) cream, and, using a fork, stir until the mixture comes together in a soft, slightly sticky dough. Turn out onto a lightly floured surface and, using your hands, bring the dough together into a ball. Gently press out into a 20cm round, then cut into 8 wedges and place, slightly apart, on baking tray. Brush tops with reserved 1 tablespoon cream, then bake for 10–12 minutes until golden.

Meanwhile, place icing sugar in a bowl and gradually add enough lemon juice to make a soft drizzle icing.

Cool the scones on a wire rack, then drizzle with icing and serve with whipped cream and lemon curd. **Makes 8**

* Lemon curd is available from delis and gourmet food shops.

Berry yoghurt muffins

1½ cups (225g) self-raising
    flour
⅓ cup (30g) rolled oats
3 eggs
¾ cup (200g) mixed berry
    yoghurt
⅓ cup (80ml) sunflower oil
1 firmly packed cup (200g)
    brown sugar
300g frozen raspberries
Icing sugar, to dust

Preheat the oven to 200°C. Grease a 6-hole, ¾-cup (185ml) capacity
Texas muffin pan.

Place the flour, oats and a pinch of salt in a bowl and mix well.

Beat the eggs, yoghurt, oil and ¾ cup (150g) brown sugar in a
bowl until combined.

Add 180g berries to the flour mixture and stir to combine. Gently
fold in the egg mixture until just combined. Spoon the mixture into
the muffin holes and bake for 20 minutes or until a skewer inserted
in the centre comes out clean.

Meanwhile, place the remaining berries and 50g brown sugar in a
saucepan with 1 tablespoon water. Cook, stirring, over low heat for
2–3 minutes until the berries soften slightly. Set the berry syrup aside
to cool slightly.

Dust the muffins with icing sugar and serve with the warm berry
syrup. **Makes 6**

Party lamingtons

85g packet strawberry jelly
   crystals
85g packet orange jelly
   crystals
1 tbs unsalted butter
1 tbs cocoa powder
½ cup (80g) pure icing sugar,
   sifted
Twin-pack (350g) square
   vanilla sponge cake*
3 cups (270g) desiccated
   coconut

Boil 2 cups (500ml) water in the kettle. Place jelly crystals in separate jugs. Pour 1 cup (250ml) of boiling water over each and use a fork to whisk until the crystals dissolve. Pour into separate shallow dishes and chill for 1–1½ hours until just starting to set. Meanwhile, place the butter, cocoa powder, icing sugar and 3 tablespoons boiling water into a shallow bowl. Stir with a fork until coating consistency.

Cut each cake into 9 squares. Spread the coconut on a large plate or a sheet of baking paper.

Dip 6 of the cake squares first in strawberry jelly, then in coconut. Place on a rack to firm slightly. Repeat with the remaining cake, dipping 6 in orange jelly and 6 in the chocolate mixture, then coconut. (If the chocolate mixture begins to set, stir in 1 tablespoon boiling water.) **Makes 18**

* Sponge cakes are available from supermarkets.

Lavender friands

1 tbs edible dried lavender
   flowers*
1⅓ cups (200g) icing sugar
60g plain flour
1 cup (125g) almond meal
5 eggwhites
180g unsalted butter,
   melted, cooled

Icing

1 tsp edible dried lavender
   flowers*
¼ cup (55g) caster sugar
⅔ cup (100g) icing sugar
Lavender food colouring*
Fresh unsprayed lavender
   flowers*, to garnish

Combine the dried lavender flowers and icing sugar, then cover
and stand for at least 3 hours, preferably overnight, to infuse.

Preheat the oven to 170°C. Line 9 holes in a friand or patty pan
with paper cases.

Place the flowers and icing sugar in a processor and process to
a fine powder, then place in a bowl with the flour and almond meal.

In a separate bowl, beat the eggwhites with a fork until frothy,
then fold into the dry mixture. Slowly fold in the butter until
combined. Divide the mixture among the friand holes, then bake
for 10–15 minutes until pale golden.

For the icing, place dried lavender flowers and caster sugar into
a spice grinder or mortar and pestle, then grind to a fine powder.
Sift the lavender sugar and the icing sugar into a bowl, then stir in
2 tablespoons warm water to make a smooth icing. Add a couple
of drops of the food colouring and stir to combine.

To serve, spread icing onto the friands and garnish each with
a small lavender flower. **Makes 9**

* Dried lavender flowers are available from delis or herbies.com.au.
Lavender food colouring is available from cake decorating shops.
Fresh lavender flowers are available from garden centres.

Coconut scones with strawberries & cream

⅓ cup (110g) strawberry jam
250g punnet strawberries,
　　halved or quartered if large
1½ cups (225g) self-raising
　　flour
1 tsp baking powder
2 tbs caster sugar
50g unsalted butter, softened
⅓ cup (30g) desiccated
　　coconut
50ml coconut cream
50ml milk, plus 1 tbs extra
　　to brush
1 egg

Mascarpone cream

100g mascarpone
1½ tbs caster sugar
150ml coconut cream
150ml thickened cream

To make the mascarpone cream, use electric beaters to mix the mascarpone in a bowl with the caster sugar and coconut cream until smooth. Whip the cream to soft peaks in a separate bowl, then gently fold through the mascarpone mixture. Cover and chill until needed.

Place jam and 2 tablespoons water in a pan over low heat, stirring until melted and combined. Add the berries and toss to coat. Set compote aside until needed.

Preheat the oven to 220°C and line a tray with baking paper. Sift the flour and baking powder into a bowl with a pinch of salt, then stir in the sugar. Rub in the butter using your fingertips, then stir in the desiccated coconut. Combine the coconut cream, milk and egg in a small bowl, then add to the dry ingredients, stirring with a knife.

Bring the mixture into a ball using your hands (do not overmix), then turn onto a lightly floured workbench and form into a 5cm-thick, 12cm-diameter round. Use a 5cm cutter to cut 4 scones from the mixture, then bring together excess and make 2 more scones. Place on the prepared tray and brush with extra milk, then bake for 10–12 minutes, until the scones have risen and the tops are golden.

Cool slightly, then split and serve with compote and mascarpone cream. **Makes 6**

Simple apricot tart

1 block of Careme All Butter
    Puff Pastry*, or 2 sheets
    butter puff pastry, joined
    then trimmed to fit
120g marzipan
2 tbs thickened cream,
    plus extra to serve
8 apricots, halved
2 tbs honey
Icing sugar and chopped
    pistachios, to serve

Preheat the oven to 200°C and line a baking tray with baking paper.

Roll out the pastry to a 20cm x 30cm rectangle and place on the baking tray. Chill for 10 minutes.

Place the marzipan and cream in a food processor and whiz until smooth. Spread over the pastry base, leaving a 2cm border. Place the apricots, cut-side up, on the marzipan mixture, then drizzle with the honey. Bake for 25 minutes or until the pastry is puffed and golden and the apricots are starting to caramelise.

Dust the tart with icing sugar and scatter with pistachios. Serve with extra cream. **Serves 4–6**

* Careme pastry is available from delis and gourmet food shops, visit: caremepastry.com

Buttermilk tart with passionfruit sauce

1 qty sweet shortcrust pastry
(see recipe, p 70), or 435g
packet Careme Vanilla
Bean Sweet Shortcrust
Pastry*
200g caster sugar
2 tbs plain flour
400ml buttermilk
3 eggs
50g unsalted butter, softened
Icing sugar, to dust

Passionfruit sauce
½ cup (110g) caster sugar
Seeds and pulp of
    4 passionfruits

Line a 23cm loose-bottomed tart pan with the pastry. Chill for 30 minutes.

Preheat the oven to 180°C. Line the pastry with baking paper and fill with pastry weights or uncooked rice, then bake for 10 minutes. Remove the paper and weights and bake for a further 5 minutes until golden and dry. Allow to cool completely.

Place the sugar, flour, buttermilk, eggs and butter in a bowl, whisking gently to combine. Pour into the cooled tart case, then bake for 45 minutes or until just set.

Meanwhile for the passionfruit sauce, place the sugar and ½ cup (125ml) water in a pan over low heat, stirring to dissolve the sugar. Increase the heat to medium-high and simmer for 5 minutes until syrupy. Stir in the passionfruit, then allow to cool.

Dust the pastry rim with icing sugar, then drizzle the passionfruit sauce over the warm tart and serve immediately. **Serves 8–10**

* Careme pastry is available from delis and gourmet food shops, visit: caremepastry.com

Rose & raspberry meringue tarts

1 quantity sweet shortcrust
   pastry (see recipe, p 70)
   or 435g packet Careme
   Vanilla Bean Sweet
   Shortcrust Pastry*
500g fresh or frozen,
   thawed raspberries,
   plus extra to serve
2 tsp rosewater*
⅓ cup (50g) arrowroot
2 tbs lemon juice
260g caster sugar
4 eggs, separated
50g unsalted butter

Grease 6 x 10cm loose-bottomed tart pans.

Roll out the pastry to 5mm thick if using homemade. Use the pastry to line the tart pans, trimming the excess. Chill while you make the filling.

Puree the raspberries in a blender, then pass through a sieve into a saucepan, pressing down with the back of a spoon to extract as much juice as possible and discarding the solids. Stir in the rosewater.

Place the arrowroot and ⅓ cup (80ml) cold water in a bowl, stirring to combine, then add to the saucepan with the lemon juice and ½ cup (110g) sugar. Place over low heat and cook, stirring, for 3–4 minutes until thick. Add the egg yolks, 1 at a time, beating well with a wooden spoon after each addition. Add the butter and stir until melted. Remove from the heat and allow to cool, then chill for 30 minutes.

Preheat the oven to 180°C.

Line the tart shells with baking paper and pastry weights or uncooked rice, then bake for 10 minutes. Remove the paper and weights, then bake for a further 5 minutes or until golden and dry. Cool, then fill the tart shells with the chilled raspberry mixture.

Beat the eggwhites with electric beaters until soft peaks form. Gradually add remaining ⅔ cup (150g) sugar, beating until stiff peaks form, then pipe or spoon over the filling. Brown meringue with a kitchen blowtorch or bake in a 200°C oven for 2–3 minutes until tinged golden. Serve with extra berries. **Serves 6**

* Careme pastry is available from delis and gourmet food shops; visit: caremepastry.com

No-pastry pear tarts

180g unsalted butter
50g plain flour
180g pure icing sugar
100g almond meal
2 tsp finely grated lemon zest
5 eggwhites
2 poached pears*, sliced
   (or 2 fresh pears, thinly
   sliced)
2 tbs flaked almonds
Icing sugar, to dust
Pure (thin) cream or ice
   cream, to serve

Preheat the oven to 200°C. Lightly grease 6 x 7cm loose-bottomed tart pans. Melt the butter in a small saucepan over medium heat for 1–2 minutes (watch closely and don't let it burn), until golden brown. Allow to cool. Sift the flour and icing sugar into a bowl and stir in the almond meal, lemon zest and melted butter. Use a fork to lightly froth the eggwhites in a separate bowl, then fold into the dry ingredients. Divide among the tart pans and place pear slices on top. Scatter with flaked almonds and bake for 10 minutes. Reduce the heat to 170°C and bake for a further 5–6 minutes or until golden. Dust with icing sugar and serve warm with cream or ice cream. **Makes 6**

* Poached pears are available from gourmet food shops.

Apple tarte Tatin

6 Granny Smith apples
1 tbs lemon juice
175g caster sugar
2 tbs pomegranate
   molasses*
1 block of Careme All Butter
   Puff Pastry*
1 tsp ground cinnamon
300ml thickened cream

Preheat the oven to 180°C.

Peel, core and quarter the apples, then toss with lemon juice. Set aside.

Place the sugar in an ovenproof frypan or Tatin dish with 2 tablespoons water over low heat, stirring until the sugar has dissolved. Increase heat to medium and cook for 3–4 minutes, swirling the pan occasionally, until a golden caramel. Remove from the heat and carefully arrange the apples in a single layer over the caramel, packing in quite tightly. Drizzle the apples with the pomegranate molasses.

Roll out pastry on a lightly floured work surface to 3–4mm thick, then place over the filling and tuck in the sides. Bake for 25 minutes or until puffed and golden. Remove from the oven and rest in the pan for 10 minutes.

Meanwhile, whisk the cinnamon and cream together until soft peaks form.

Invert the tarte Tatin onto a serving plate and serve with the cinnamon cream. **Serves 6**

* Pomegranate molasses has a sweet, sour flavour and is available from selected supermarkets and delis. Careme pastry is available from delis and gourmet food shops; visit: caremepastry.com

Little fig & rosewater pies

450g packet frozen sour
   cream shortcrust pastry*
   (or use 4 sheets butter puff
   pastry), thawed
4 fresh figs
4 sugar cubes
2 tsp rosewater*
1 egg, lightly beaten
Icing sugar, to dust
Pure (thin) cream, to serve

Preheat the oven to 200°C. Line a baking tray with paper. Roll out the pastry on a lightly floured surface to 5mm thick. Cut 4 x 10cm and 4 x 12cm circles from the pastry.

Trim the stalk from each fig, then turn over. Cut a cross in the base, then squash down a little with your hand to flatten and open out slightly. Press a sugar cube into the cross of each fig and sprinkle with the rosewater.

Sit each fig right-way up in the centre of the larger pastry rounds and brush the border with beaten egg. Cover with the smaller pastry rounds, then fold in the edges of the larger pieces and pinch the edges to seal. Place on the lined tray. (You can keep the tarts chilled at this stage for 3–4 hours until ready to bake.)

Just before baking, brush the pies all over with beaten egg, then cook in the oven for 25 minutes or until the pastry is golden and the fig juices are starting to ooze.

Dust the warm pies with icing sugar and serve with cream.

Makes 4

* Sour cream pastry is available from delis and gourmet food shops. Rosewater is available from Middle Eastern and gourmet food shops.

Lazy lemon tart

1 quantity sweet shortcrust
   pastry (see recipe, p 70) or
   435g packet Careme
   Vanilla Bean Sweet
   Shortcrust Pastry*
1 large lemon, seeds
   removed, chopped
1½ cups (330g) caster sugar
110g softened unsalted
   butter
1 tsp vanilla extract
4 eggs
¼ cup (60ml) thickened cream
Icing sugar and thick cream,
   to serve

Grease a 23cm loose-bottomed tart pan. Roll out pastry on a lightly floured surface to 5mm thick and use to line tart pan. Refrigerate for 30 minutes.

Preheat the oven to 190°C. Line tart case with baking paper and fill with rice or pastry weights. Bake for 8 minutes, remove paper and weights, then bake for a further 3 minutes or until dry and crisp.

Meanwhile, place lemon, sugar, butter, vanilla and eggs in a high-speed blender. Blend until smooth, add thickened cream and pulse quickly to just combine. Pour lemon mixture into tart shell, then bake for 30 minutes or until just set. Cool tart in pan, then dust with icing sugar and serve at room temperature with thick cream.
Serves 6–8

* Careme pastry is available from delis and gourmet food shops; visit: caremepastry.com

Salted macadamia & caramel tarts

1 eggwhite, lightly whisked
300g jar dulce de leche*
⅔ cup (100g) salted
   macadamias, lightly
   toasted
Icing sugar, to dust
Melted chocolate, to drizzle

Sweet shortcrust pastry*
1½ cups (225g) plain flour
125g chilled unsalted butter,
   chopped
⅓ cup (50g) icing sugar
1 tsp vanilla extract
1 egg yolk

To make sweet shortcrust pastry, process flour, butter and icing sugar in a food processor to fine breadcrumbs. Add vanilla, egg yolk and 1 tbs iced water, then process until the mixture just comes together. Form into a ball, then enclose in plastic wrap and refrigerate for 30 minutes.

Grease 6 x 10cm loose-bottomed tart pans. Roll out pastry on a lightly floured surface to 5mm thick and used to line tart pans. Refrigerate for 15 minutes.

Preheat the oven to 190°C. Prick pastry bases with a fork, then line with baking paper and fill with rice or pastry weights. Bake for 10 minutes, then remove paper and weights.

Brush the insides of the pastry bases with eggwhite, then return to the oven for a further 2–3 minutes until golden, dry and crisp. Set aside to cool.

Fill the cooled tart bases with dulce de leche, then divide macadamias among the tarts. Dust with icing sugar and drizzle with melted chocolate to serve. **Serves 6**

* Dulce de leche is a South American milk caramel, available in jars from selected delis, supermarkets and gourmet food shops; see recipe, p 38. As an alternative to homemade pastry, use store-bought shortcrust pastry or sweet shortcrust pastry; Careme Vanilla Bean Sweet Shortcrust Pastry is available from gourmet food shops and selected delis; visit caremepastry.com

Chocolate silk tart
with chocolate glace oranges

1 cup (220g) caster sugar
2 seedless oranges,
    thinly sliced
400g dark chocolate,
    chopped, plus 100g melted
1 qty shop-bought chocolate
    pastry or sweet shortcrust
    pastry*
400ml pure (thin) cream
3 eggs, lightly beaten
¼ cup (60ml) Grand Marnier
    or other orange liqueur

Chocolate glaze

⅓ cup (80ml) pure (thin)
    cream
100g dark chocolate,
    chopped
2 tsp liquid glucose or honey

Preheat oven to 120°C. Line a large baking tray with baking paper.

To make chocolate glace oranges, place sugar and 1 cup (250ml) water in a saucepan. Stir over low heat until sugar dissolves, then increase heat to medium and simmer for a further 2–3 minutes until slightly reduced. Remove from heat, add orange slices and set aside to cool completely. Transfer orange slices to the lined baking tray and place in oven for 4 hours until crisp and dry. Half-dip each slice in melted chocolate and cool on a wire rack.

Meanwhile, increase the oven to 190°C. Grease a 20cm x 30cm loose-bottomed tart pan.

Roll out pastry to 5mm thick and use to line tart pan. Refrigerate for 30 minutes. Prick tart base with a fork, then line with baking paper and fill with rice or pastry weights. Bake for 10 minutes, then remove paper and weights, and cook for a further 2 minutes or until crisp and dry. Reduce the oven to 170°C.

Place cream in a saucepan over medium heat and bring to just below boiling point. Place chocolate in a bowl and pour over cream. Stand until chocolate melts, then stir until smooth. Add eggs and liqueur, then stir to combine. Pour into tart shell, then bake for 20 minutes or until just set. Cool in pan.

To make glaze, heat cream in a small saucepan over low heat for 1–2 minutes until hot. Place the chocolate and glucose in a bowl, then pour over cream. Stand until chocolate melts, then stir until smooth. Cool slightly, then pour over tart, tilting tart to spread glaze evenly. Refrigerate for 15 minutes to set glaze.

Serve the chocolate tart with chocolate glace oranges. **Serves 8**

* Careme Vanilla Bean Sweet Shortcrust Pastry is available from gourmet food shops and selected delis; visit: caremepastry.com

Key lime pie with macadamia crust

300g shortbread biscuits

⅓ cup (50g) roasted
   macadamias

½ cup (45g) desiccated
   coconut

125g unsalted butter, melted

4 eggs, separated

395g can sweetened
   condensed milk

Finely grated zest
   and juice of 4 limes

¼ cup (55g) caster sugar

Icing sugar, melted dark
   chocolate and raspberries,
   to serve

Preheat the oven to 180°C and grease a 24cm loose-bottomed tart pan.

Place the biscuits, macadamias and coconut in a food processor and whiz to fine crumbs. Add the butter and pulse a few times to combine. Press the biscuit mixture into the base and sides of the tart pan, then chill for 10 minutes to firm up.

Bake the biscuit base for 10 minutes or until golden, then allow to cool slightly.

Meanwhile, place the egg yolks, condensed milk and lime zest and juice in a bowl and beat with a wooden spoon to combine.

In a separate bowl, beat the eggwhites with electric beaters until frothy. Add the caster sugar, 1 tablespoon at a time, beating constantly until soft peaks form. Fold the eggwhite mixture into the yolk mixture, then pour into the tart case.

Bake for 35 minutes or until the filling is just set. Remove from the oven and cool – the filling will deflate slightly. Chill for 1 hour.

Dust the pie with icing sugar and drizzle with chocolate. Serve with raspberries. **Serves 6–8**

Peach tartes fines with pink pepper ice cream

1L good-quality vanilla
  ice cream
1 tbs pink peppercorns*,
  crushed, plus extra
  to serve
½ cup (110g) caster sugar
2 bay leaves
1 vanilla bean, split
6 yellow peaches (preferably
  slipstone)
2 sheets frozen puff pastry,
  thawed
Icing sugar, to dust

Soften ice cream slightly and stir through crushed peppercorns, then return to freezer until ready to serve.

Place caster sugar, bay leaves and vanilla in a saucepan with 4 cups (1L) water and bring to a simmer over medium-high heat, stirring until sugar dissolves. Add peaches, cover surface closely with a round of baking paper (cartouche), then reduce heat to medium-low and simmer for 5–10 minutes until tender (depending on the firmness of your peaches). Remove pan from heat and cool peaches in poaching liquid.

Preheat the oven to 180°C. Line a heavy-based baking tray with baking paper.

Cut 6 x 12cm rounds from pastry and place on lined baking tray. Prick bases with a fork, then refrigerate until ready to assemble tarts.

Meanwhile, remove peaches from liquid and pat dry, then halve, remove stone and thinly slice. Fan out each sliced peach, slightly overlapping, over pastry rounds. Dust with icing sugar, then bake for 20 minutes or until the edges of the peaches are golden and pastry is crisp and cooked through.

Serve with pink peppercorn ice cream, scattered with extra peppercorns. **Serves 6**

* Pink peppercorns are available from spice shops and selected gourmet food shops, or online at essentialingredient.com.au or herbies.com.au

Greek apple pie

½ cup (110g) caster sugar
1 cinnamon quill
1 vanilla bean, split
½ cup (80g) sultanas
2 Granny Smith apples,
   peeled, cored,
   cut into 2cm pieces,
   to give 3 cups (500g)
   chopped apple
2 tbs maple syrup,
   plus extra to drizzle
½ cup (60g) finely chopped
   walnuts
1 tsp ground cinnamon
¼ cup (60g) brown sugar
8 sheets filo pastry
80g unsalted butter, melted,
   cooled
2 tbs chopped pistachio
   kernels
Icing sugar, to dust

Preheat the oven to 180°C. Grease a 24cm springform cake pan.

Place caster sugar, cinnamon quill, vanilla and sultanas in a saucepan with 1 cup (250ml) water. Bring to a simmer over medium-low heat, stirring until sugar dissolves, then cook for 10 minutes or until reduced. Add apple and cook for a further 6–8 minutes until tender. Add maple syrup, stir to combine, then set aside to cool.

Combine walnuts, ground cinnamon and brown sugar in a bowl.

Working with 1 sheet of filo at a time and keeping the others covered with a lightly dampened tea towel to prevent them from drying out, lightly brush filo sheet with melted butter. Sprinkle with a quarter of the nut mixture, top with another filo sheet, brush with butter and spread a quarter of the apple mixture along the long edge. Roll up from the long edge and brush with butter, then repeat with remaining mixture and filo until you have 4 rolls. Coil rolls in pan to form a spiral (if rolls crack, patch with extra filo brushed with butter).

Bake for 25 minutes or until golden. To serve, drizzle with extra maple syrup, scatter over pistachios and dust with icing sugar.

Serves 6

Still-life tart

1 king mushroom
1 spring onion
2 tsp olive oil
1 cup (250g) mascarpone
150g soft goat's cheese
20g unsalted butter, softened
3 eggs
300ml thickened cream
About 10 enoki mushrooms
3 dill sprigs

Pastry

1⅔ cups (250g) plain flour
125g chilled unsalted
    butter, chopped
2 egg yolks

For the pastry, place flour and butter in a food processor with ½ teaspoon salt and whiz until fine crumbs. Add egg yolks and ¼ cup (60ml) iced water. Process until the mixture comes together in a smooth ball. Enclose in plastic wrap and chill for 30 minutes.

Lightly grease a 27cm x 19cm loose-bottomed tart pan. Roll the pastry out on a lightly floured surface until 5mm thick, then use it to line the tart pan. Chill for a further 30 minutes.

Preheat the oven to 180°C.

Line the pastry case with baking paper and fill with pastry weights or uncooked rice. Bake for 10 minutes, then remove weights and paper and bake for a further 3 minutes until pastry is golden and dry. Set aside.

Slice the king mushroom lengthways and place on a baking tray with the spring onion. Brush with the oil and roast for 5–6 minutes until the spring onion begins to wilt. Set aside.

Meanwhile, place mascarpone, goat's cheese, butter, eggs and cream in a food processor and whiz until smooth. Season, then pour into the tart case and bake for 10 minutes or until just starting to set. Arrange the king and enoki mushrooms, spring onion and dill sprigs on top of the tart and bake for a further 15 minutes or until the filling is set. Serve warm. **Serves 4–6**

Onion & bacon tart with parmesan cream

1 tbs olive oil

4 onions, thinly sliced

2 tbs brown sugar

2 tbs balsamic vinegar

1 pkt frozen Careme Puff
  Pastry*, thawed

4 thin bacon rashers

1 tbs thyme leaves

1 egg, lightly beaten

Parmesan cream

20g unsalted butter

4 spring onions, thinly sliced

100ml thickened cream

100g grated parmesan

Preheat the oven to 200°C.

Line a large baking tray with baking paper.

Heat the oil in a large frypan over medium-low heat. Add the onion and cook for 5–6 minutes, stirring occasionally, until softened. Add the sugar and balsamic and continue to cook for 4–5 minutes until dark and caramelised. Cool completely.

Roll out pastry to 2–3mm thick, then cut a 25cm circle. Score a 2cm border around the edge, then place the pastry on the prepared tray. Spread the caramelised onions over the pastry, taking care not to go over the border. Top with bacon, scatter with half the thyme, then brush the exposed edge with the egg. Bake in the oven for 20 minutes or until puffed and golden.

Meanwhile, to make the parmesan cream, melt the butter in a small saucepan over medium-low heat. Add spring onion and cook for 1–2 minutes until soft. Add cream and remaining thyme and bring to a simmer, then cook for 2–3 minutes until slightly reduced. Stir in the parmesan and season to taste. Cool slightly, then puree in a blender until smooth. (This can be made 2 days in advance, then gently reheated before serving.)

Drizzle the parmesan cream over the tart, then slice and serve.

Serves 4–6

* Careme pastry is available from delis and gourmet food shops, visit: caremepastry.com

Asparagus & ricotta tart

1 egg
250g fresh ricotta, well
   drained
¼ cup (60ml) pure (thin)
   cream
¼ cup (60ml) milk
¼ cup basil leaves
2 tbs chopped chives
2 bunches asparagus,
   woody ends trimmed
Micro herbs or extra basil,
   to serve

Shortcrust pastry*
1½ cups (225g) plain flour
125g chilled unsalted butter,
   chopped
1 egg yolk

Preheat the oven to 200°C and grease a 30cm x 20cm rectangular loose-bottomed tart pan.

To make the pastry, whiz the flour, butter and a pinch of salt in a food processor to fine crumbs. Add the egg yolk and 2 tablespoons chilled water and whiz until the mixture just comes together. Shape into a ball, enclose in plastic wrap, then chill for 30 minutes before rolling out.

Roll out the pastry to 5mm thick if using homemade. Line the tart pan, trimming the excess. Chill for 10 minutes.

Line the pastry with baking paper and fill with pastry weights or uncooked rice. Bake for 10 minutes, then remove the paper and weights. Bake for a further 3 minutes or until golden and dry. Cool slightly.

Reduce the oven to 180°C.

Place the egg, ricotta, cream, milk, basil and chives in a food processor, season, then whiz to combine. Spread the ricotta mixture into the tart shell, then arrange the asparagus spears on top.

Bake for 25 minutes or until the filling is set. Cool slightly, then cut the tart into slices and serve scattered with herbs. **Serves 4–6**

* The pastry will keep in the freezer for up to one month. Alternatively use shop-bought shortcrust pastry; Careme Sour Cream Shortcrust Pastry is available from delis and gourmet food shops, visit caremepastry.com

Duck & shiitake mushroom pithiviers

50g dried shiitake
　　mushrooms*, soaked
　　in boiling water for
　　15 minutes
1 tbs olive oil
1 onion, finely chopped
1 tbs grated ginger
2 garlic cloves, crushed
2 tsp plain flour
1 tsp five-spice powder
1 tbs soy sauce
1 Chinese barbecued duck*,
　　meat cut into small pieces,
　　skin and bones discarded
4 sheets frozen puff pastry,
　　thawed
1 egg, lightly beaten
Spring onion & ginger sauce*
　　and plum sauce*, to serve

Drain the mushrooms, reserving ½ cup (125ml) of the soaking liquid, then chop.

Heat the oil in a frypan over medium heat. Add the onion and cook, stirring, for 2–3 minutes until soft. Add the ginger, garlic and mushrooms and cook, stirring, for 1–2 minutes. Add the flour and five-spice, stir to combine, then add the reserved soaking liquid and cook, stirring, for 2 minutes or until the sauce thickens. Stir in the soy and duck, then season with salt to taste. Remove from the heat and allow to cool.

Preheat the oven to 180°C. Using a 12cm cutter, cut 4 rounds from each pastry sheet. Place 8 rounds on a large lined baking tray. Divide filling among the pastry rounds, leaving a 1.5cm border. Brush edges with a little egg, then top with remaining pastry and press to seal. Use a small sharp knife to lightly score a 1cm border around the edge of each pithivier and a spiral pattern over the top. Brush with more beaten egg, then bake for 25 minutes or until puffed and golden. Serve with the spring onion and plum sauces.
Makes 8

* Dried shiitakes are available from Asian food shops. Chinese barbecued duck is available from Asian barbecue shops. Spring onion & ginger sauce and plum sauce are available from selected supermarkets and Asian food shops.

Heirloom tomato pastry tarts

1 sheet frozen puff
   pastry, thawed
⅓ cup (80g) fresh ricotta
2 tbs (40g) mascarpone
2 tbs finely grated parmesan
1 egg, lightly beaten
2 tsp thyme leaves
200g heirloom cherry
   tomatoes*
Rocket leaves and balsamic
   vinegar, to serve

Preheat the oven to 180°C. Line a baking tray with baking paper.

Using a 10cm heart-shaped pastry cutter, cut the pastry into 4 hearts. Carefully cut a 2cm border into 2 hearts, then discard the inner pastry heart, reserving the heart-shaped borders. Brush the borders with water, then arrange the borders, watered-side down, on top of the whole pastry hearts, gently pressing down to seal. Transfer to the baking tray and set aside.

Combine ricotta, mascarpone, parmesan and most of the egg. Season, then stir in the thyme leaves. Spoon the cheese mixture into the centre of the hearts and place the tomatoes on top. Use the remaining egg to brush the pastry border.

Bake for 8–10 minutes until pastry is golden and the filling is set. Scatter with rocket, drizzle with balsamic vinegar and serve.
Serves 2

* Heirloom cherry tomatoes are available from farmers' markets and selected greengrocers.

Chicken & Taleggio jalousie

50g unsalted butter

1 tbs olive oil

1 leek (white part only),
   thinly sliced

250g Swiss brown
   mushrooms, sliced

2 tsp chopped thyme leaves

2 tsp plain flour

½ cup (125ml) chicken stock

½ cup (125ml) thickened
   cream

2½ cups (400g) shredded
   cooked chicken

1 pkt frozen Careme Puff
   Pastry*, thawed

150g Taleggio or other
   washed rind cheese,
   rind removed, chopped

1 egg, lightly beaten

Place the butter and oil in a frypan over medium-low heat. Add the leek and cook, stirring, for 5 minutes or until softened. Add the mushroom and thyme, then cook, stirring, for 1–2 minutes until softened. Add the flour and cook, stirring, for 1 minute, then stir in the stock and cream. Cook for 1–2 minutes until the sauce is slightly thickened, then stir in the chicken and season well. Set aside to cool.

Preheat the oven to 200°C. Line a baking tray with baking paper.

Roll out the pastry on a lightly floured surface to a 20cm x 40cm rectangle, then cut in half lengthways. Place 1 pastry half on the baking tray, then spread over chicken filling, leaving a 1cm border. Scatter with Taleggio and brush the pastry edges with egg.

Gently fold the remaining pastry in half lengthways. Use a sharp knife to make cuts at 1cm intervals down the folded side, leaving a 1cm border on the other side. Carefully open up the folded pastry and place over the filling, pressing the edges to seal – the pastry should separate slightly to reveal some of the filling. Brush all over with beaten egg and bake for 25 minutes or until puffed and golden. Cut into slices and serve. **Serves 4–6**

* Careme pastry is available from delis and gourmet food shops, visit: caremepastry.com

Spicy crab tarts

2 large frozen shortcrust
    pastry sheets, thawed
200ml pure (thin) cream
1 egg, plus 1 extra yolk
1 long red chilli, seeds
    removed, finely chopped
2 tsp grated ginger
200g fresh crabmeat*,
    drained
2 spring onions, thinly sliced
2 tbs chopped coriander
    leaves
Baby herb salad and chilli oil*
    (optional), to serve

Preheat the oven to 180°C and grease 8 x 10cm loose-bottomed tart pans.

Use a 12cm cutter to cut 4 rounds from each pastry sheet, then use to line the tart pans. Chill for 10 minutes.

Line the pastry with baking paper and fill with pastry weights or uncooked rice. Place the pans on a tray and bake for 8 minutes. Remove the paper and pastry weights or rice, then bake the tart shells for a further 3 minutes until light golden.

Meanwhile, whisk the cream, egg and yolk in a bowl. Add the chilli and ginger, season with salt and pepper and mix well to combine.

Divide the crabmeat, spring onion and coriander among the tart shells. Pour over the egg mixture. Bake for 15 minutes or until the filling is just set. Serve with herb salad and a drizzle of chilli oil if desired. **Makes 8**

* Fresh crabmeat is available from fishmongers. Chilli oil is available from Asian and gourmet food shops.

Cheese & fig tarts

3 sheets frozen shortcrust
   pastry, thawed
150g soft goat's cheese
1 cup (240g) ricotta
¼ cup (20g) grated parmesan
3 eggs
½ cup (125ml) pure
   (thin) cream
1 tbs rosemary leaves,
   chopped
3 figs, halved
Vincotto* and micro herbs*,
   to serve

Line 6 x 10cm-wide, 3cm-deep loose-bottomed tart pans with
the pastry, trimming any excess. Refrigerate for 30 minutes.

Preheat the oven to 180°C.

Prick the pastry with a fork, then line with baking paper and fill
with pastry weights or uncooked rice. Bake for 10 minutes, then
remove paper and weights. Bake for a further 2 minutes or until
the pastry is golden and dry.

Meanwhile, beat goat's cheese, ricotta, parmesan, eggs and
cream together, then season. Stir in the rosemary, then divide
among the tart cases. Press a fig half, cut-side up, into the filling.
Bake for 20–25 minutes until the filling is just set.

Drizzle the tarts with vincotto and garnish with the micro herbs.
Serve warm. **Makes 6**

* Vincotto is available from Italian delis and gourmet food shops;
substitute balsamic glaze. Micro herbs are available from farmers'
markets and selected greengrocers.

Chicken, leek & bacon pot pies

40g unsalted butter

1 tbs olive oil

3 leeks (pale part only), thinly
sliced

4 bacon rashers, rind
removed, chopped

800g chicken thigh fillets, cut
into 2cm pieces

1 tbs plain flour

Pinch of nutmeg

200ml chicken stock

300ml light sour cream or
creme fraiche

2 tbs chopped flat-leaf
parsley

2 tbs lemon juice

4 sheets frozen puff pastry,
thawed

1 egg, lightly beaten

Heat the butter and oil in a pan over low heat. Add the leek, bacon and chicken and cook, stirring, for 6–8 minutes until the leek is soft and chicken is almost cooked. Stir in the flour and nutmeg and cook for 1–2 minutes until the chicken is cooked through. Stir in the stock, increase heat to medium and bring to the boil. Season, then remove from the heat and stir in the sour cream, parsley and lemon juice. Cool completely.

Preheat the oven to 200°C.

Cut two 1cm strips from the sides of each pastry sheet. Set aside. Cut pie lids from the remaining pastry, 1cm wider than the top of 4 x 300ml pie dishes or ramekins. Divide chicken mixture among dishes. Press pastry strips around the rim of each dish to make a 'collar' and brush with some of the egg. Carefully top with pie lids, press firmly into the collar to seal, then trim edges if necessary. Make 2 cuts in each pie top, then brush with remaining egg. Bake the pies for 20 minutes or until puffed and golden. **Serves 4**

Pumpkin & leek tart with pan-fried mushrooms

700g pumpkin, peeled,
cut into 3cm-thick slices

1 tbs olive oil

1 qty savoury shortcrust
pastry (see recipe p 84)

40g unsalted butter

2 leeks (white part only),
thinly sliced

3 garlic cloves, roughly
chopped

¼ cup (60ml) dry white wine

300ml pure (thin) cream

2 eggs, plus 1 egg yolk

2 tsp chopped thyme leaves

2 tbs chopped flat-leaf parsley

1 cup (125g) grated gruyere
cheese

Pinch of freshly grated
nutmeg

Pan-fried mushrooms

40g unsalted butter

2 garlic cloves, finely chopped

400g mixed wild mushrooms*
(such as pine, chestnut and
shiitake)

¼ cup (60ml) dry white wine

2 tbs chopped flat-leaf parsley

Preheat the oven to 180°C. Line a baking tray with baking paper and grease a 26cm loose-bottomed tart pan. Place pumpkin on the tray, drizzle with olive oil and season with salt and pepper. Cover the tray with foil and roast in the oven for 25 minutes or until pumpkin is soft. Place pumpkin in a sieve over a bowl and allow to drain for 30 minutes.

Meanwhile, roll out pastry on a lightly floured surface to 5mm thick, then use to line the tart pan. Chill for 15 minutes, then line with baking paper and fill with pastry weights or uncooked rice. Bake in oven for 10 minutes, then remove paper and weights and cook for a further 5 minutes or until golden and dry.

Meanwhile, melt butter in a large frypan over medium-low heat. Add the leek and garlic and cook, stirring, for 3–4 minutes until leek softens. Add the wine and reduce for 2–3 minutes until most of the liquid has evaporated, then cool slightly. Place the pumpkin, leek mixture, cream, eggs, yolk, thyme and parsley in a food processor and process until smooth. Stir in the cheese and nutmeg, then season well. Pour pumpkin mixture into tart shell, then bake for 40 minutes until firm and golden.

Meanwhile for the mushrooms, heat butter in a pan over medium heat. Add garlic and mushrooms and cook, stirring, for 2–3 minutes until mushrooms have wilted. Add wine and allow to bubble for 2–3 minutes until wine has evaporated and mushrooms are tender. Toss with parsley, then scatter over tart and serve. **Serves 4–6**

* Wild mushrooms are available from selected greengrocers and farmers' markets.

Toad in the hole with mustard & onion gravy

¾ cup (110g) plain flour,
  sifted, plus 1 tbs extra

3 eggs

300ml milk

1 tbs finely chopped chives

1 tbs finely chopped flat-leaf
  parsley leaves

2 tbs sunflower oil

8 pork chipolata sausages

1 large red onion,
  cut into thin wedges

1 tbs wholegrain mustard

2 tbs thyme leaves

300ml beef stock

1 tsp Worcestershire sauce

1 tbs redcurrant jelly

½ tsp tomato paste

Preheat oven to 180°C.

Place the flour, eggs, milk, chives, parsley and 1 teaspoon salt in a bowl and whisk to combine. Stand the batter for 15 minutes.

Place 1 tablespoon oil in a frypan over medium-high heat. Cook the chipolatas, turning, for 4–5 minutes until well browned and almost cooked through.

Remove chipolatas from the pan and roughly chop. Divide the chipolatas and any oil from the frypan among 4 x 1½-cup (375ml) pie dishes (or use 8 holes of 2 Texas muffin pans). Pour in the batter, filling the pie dishes or muffin holes to three-quarters full. Bake for 20 minutes or until puffed and golden.

Meanwhile, place the remaining 1 tablespoon oil in the frypan and place over medium heat. Add the onion to the pan and cook, stirring occasionally, for 3–4 minutes until soft and golden. Sprinkle the extra 1 tablespoon flour over the onion, stirring to combine, then add the mustard, thyme, stock, Worcestershire, redcurrant jelly and tomato paste. Cook, whisking occasionally, for 3–4 minutes until thickened and combined.

Serve the toad in the hole immediately with the mustard and onion gravy. **Serves 4**

Salmon, egg & dill pie

½ cup (100g) basmati
  or long-grain rice
⅓ cup (80ml) thickened
  cream
30g unsalted butter, chopped
1 tbs finely chopped dill
1 tbs finely chopped flat-leaf
  parsley leaves
Finely grated zest of 1 lemon
1 pkt frozen Careme Puff
  Pastry*, thawed
300g hot-smoked salmon
  fillets, skin removed, flaked
3 eggs, soft-boiled,
  quartered, plus 1 lightly
  beaten egg, to brush

Caper butter sauce

120g unsalted butter,
  chopped
2 tbs baby capers, rinsed
2 tbs chopped dill

To make filling, cook rice in boiling salted water for 8 minutes or until just cooked. Rinse under cold running water, then drain well. Transfer to a bowl with the cream, butter, dill, parsley and lemon zest, then season with sea salt and freshly ground black pepper and stir to combine.

Divide pastry in half and roll out 1 portion to a 25cm x 30cm rectangle. Place on a baking tray lined with baking paper and spread over half the rice mixture. Top with salmon, then soft-boiled egg. Brush pastry edges with water, then spread remaining rice over filling. Roll out remaining pastry to a 25cm x 30cm rectangle, then cut with a lattice cutter (available from kitchenware shops). Place on top of rice mixture, pressing edges to seal. Alternatively, roll out remaining portion of pastry to a 25cm x 30cm rectangle and place over filling, pressing edges to seal. Refrigerate pie for 30 minutes.

Preheat the oven to 180°C. Brush top of pastry with beaten egg, then bake pie for 25–30 minutes until puffed and golden.

To make caper butter sauce, melt butter, without stirring, in a frypan over low heat, skimming any foam from surface. Remove from heat and stand for 1 minute or until milk solids sink to bottom. Carefully pour liquid clarified butter into a jug, discarding solids. Stir in capers and dill.

Slice pie and serve with the warm caper butter sauce. **Serves 6**

* Careme pastry is available from delis and gourmet food shops, visit: caremepastry.com

Quail egg & pancetta tart

1 pkt frozen Careme Puff
   Pastry*, thawed
100ml creme fraiche or
   sour cream
2 tbs grated parmesan
150g thinly sliced pancetta
8 quail eggs* or 5 small eggs
Chervil sprigs* or flat-leaf
   parsley leaves, to garnish

Preheat oven to 180°C. Line a baking tray with baking paper.

Roll out the pastry on a lightly floured surface to form a 16cm x 30cm rectangle. Place the pastry on the prepared baking tray. Use a knife to lightly score a 1cm border around the edge of the pastry, taking care not to cut all the way through.

Prick the area inside the border with a fork.

Mix creme fraiche and parmesan in a bowl and season with salt and pepper. Spread the mixture over the pastry inside the border. Lay pancetta over the tart base, then bake for 12 minutes or until the pancetta is crisp and the pastry is puffed and golden.

Lightly beat 1 egg. Remove the pastry from the oven and brush the border with the beaten egg. Break the remaining eggs, one at a time, into a cup and pour over the pancetta.

Season with salt and pepper, then return to the oven for a further 3 minutes or until the eggwhites are set but yolks are still runny. Scatter with chervil or parsley, then slice and serve. **Serves 6**

* Careme pastry is available from delis and gourmet food shops, visit: caremepastry.com. Quail eggs are available from selected poultry suppliers and Asian food shops. Chervil is available from selected greengrocers.

Molten mocha puddings

150g good-quality dark
   chocolate, finely chopped
125g unsalted butter,
   chopped
3 tsp instant espresso coffee
2 eggs, plus 2 extra yolks
½ cup (75g) pure icing sugar,
   sifted
¼ cup (35g) plain flour, sifted
2 tsp cocoa powder, sifted
Fresh strawberries, halved,
   to serve

Preheat the oven to 200°C. Grease a 6-hole, ¾-cup (185ml) capacity Texas muffin pan.

Place the chocolate, butter and coffee in a saucepan over low heat, stirring until melted and smooth. Remove from the heat and set aside to cool for 10 minutes.

Use electric beaters to beat the eggs, egg yolks and icing sugar together in a bowl until thick and pale. Gently fold in the flour and cooled chocolate mixture.

Spoon mixture into the muffin holes and bake for 10–12 minutes until the puddings look firm on the outside but are molten on the inside when pierced with a skewer. Set aside for 2–3 minutes to rest in the pan, then invert onto plates. Dust with cocoa powder and serve with strawberries. **Makes 6**

Lemon meringue bread & butter pudding

50g unsalted butter, softened

1 cup (325g) good-quality
  lemon curd*

10 white bread slices,
  crusts removed

1½ cups (375ml) milk

½ cup (125ml) pure (thin)
  cream, plus extra to serve

Finely grated zest of 1 lemon

4 eggs, separated,
  plus 1 extra eggwhite

185g caster sugar

Spread the butter and lemon curd on one side of each bread slice. Cut in half on the diagonal to make 20 triangles, then arrange in a greased 1L baking dish, overlapping slightly and forming 2 layers.

Place the milk, cream and zest in a saucepan over medium heat and bring to just below boiling point. Remove from heat and stand for 10 minutes to infuse.

Preheat the oven to 170°C.

Place the egg yolks and ½ cup (110g) sugar in a bowl and beat with electric beaters until thick and pale. Slowly pour in the milk mixture, beating to combine. Strain, then pour over the bread. Stand for 15 minutes to allow the custard to soak in.

Bake the pudding for 30 minutes or until just set.

Meanwhile, place all the eggwhites in a clean, dry bowl and whisk with electric beaters until soft peaks form. Gradually add the remaining ⅓ cup (75g) sugar, whisking constantly, until glossy and stiff peaks form.

Increase the oven temperature to 200°C.

Spread the meringue over the top of the pudding using the back of a spoon, then return to the oven and bake for 6–8 minutes until meringue is tinged golden. Serve warm with extra cream. **Serves 6**

* Lemon curd is available from delis and gourmet food shops.

Surprise raspberry souffles

25g unsalted butter, melted,
  cooled, to brush
⅓ cup (75g) caster sugar, plus
  extra to dust
3 x 125g punnets raspberries
5 eggwhites
6 shop-bought undusted
  chocolate truffles
Icing sugar and shaved
  chocolate curls, to serve

Preheat the oven to 200°C. Working in upward brushstrokes from the bottom to the top of each ramekin, brush 6 x 200ml ramekins with melted butter, then liberally dust with extra caster sugar, gently tapping ramekins to remove excess sugar.

Process raspberries in a food processor, then press through a sieve, discarding solids, to give 1 cup (250ml) puree. Add 1 tablespoon caster sugar and stir until sugar dissolves.

Using electric beaters, whisk eggwhites to soft peaks. Whisking constantly, slowly add remaining ¼ cup (55g) caster sugar and whisk to stiff peaks. Gently fold a quarter of the eggwhite mixture into puree to loosen, then fold in the remaining eggwhite mixture. Using a piping bag, if possible, pipe raspberry mixture to half fill the ramekins. Add a truffle to each one, then pipe raspberry mixture on top to fill to the rim of the ramekin. Smooth top with a palette knife, then run your thumb gently around the inside of the ramekins (this will help the souffles to rise). Bake for 7 minutes or until well risen and golden on top.

Serve souffles dusted with icing sugar and topped with chocolate curls. **Serves 6**

Lemon curd profiteroles

1 cup (250ml) milk

110g unsalted butter

2 tsp caster sugar

1 cup (150g) plain flour, sifted

5 large (70g) eggs, lightly
   beaten

200g mascarpone cheese

200g good-quality lemon
   curd*

Icing sugar, to dust

Lemon syrup

Finely grated zest of
   3 lemons, plus 100ml juice

100g caster sugar

Preheat the oven to 220°C and line 2 large baking trays.

Place the milk in a saucepan with ½ cup (125ml) water, butter, sugar and a pinch of salt over medium heat. Bring to just below boiling point, then reduce the heat to low. Quickly add flour and beat with a wooden spoon until the mixture is well combined. Transfer to an electric mixer and add the eggs one at a time, beating well after each addition, until completely incorporated.

Spoon the batter into a piping bag fitted with a plain nozzle. In batches, if necessary, pipe 3cm rounds of batter onto the trays, spaced 2cm apart. (If you don't have a piping bag, use 2 teaspoons to drop rounds onto the tray.) You should have about 50 profiteroles. Bake for 12 minutes, then turn the oven off and leave them to dry in the oven, with the door slightly ajar, for 15 minutes. Remove from the oven and leave to cool for 30 minutes, then repeat with the remaining batter if needed.

For the syrup, place lemon zest, juice and sugar in a pan over low heat. Stir to dissolve sugar, then simmer for 5 minutes, without stirring, until syrupy. Allow to cool completely. Meanwhile, beat mascarpone and lemon curd with electric beaters until thick. Chill.

To assemble, split each profiterole in half, pipe or spoon the lemon curd filling onto the profiterole bases, then return tops to cover. Pile onto a cake stand, then drizzle with the lemon syrup and dust with icing sugar just before serving. **Makes 50**

* Lemon curd is available from delis and gourmet food shops.

Three milks cake

3 eggs, separated
1 tbs vanilla extract
200g golden caster sugar*
1 cup (150g) self-raising flour,
    sifted
1 tsp baking powder
½ cup (125ml)
    evaporated milk
½ cup (125ml)
    condensed milk
½ cup (125ml)
    full-cream milk
200ml thickened cream,
    whipped to soft peaks
Seasonal berries, to serve

Preheat the oven to 150°C. Grease and line base and side of a 20cm springform cake pan.

Using an electric mixer, whisk eggwhites on low speed for 1 minute or until frothy. Add egg yolks and beat on medium speed for 1 minute. Add vanilla and sugar, and beat for 1 minute. Add flour and baking powder, and beat for a further 1 minute or until just combined. Transfer batter to cake pan, gently smoothing surface, then bake for 35–40 minutes until golden. Cool cake in pan for 15–20 minutes, then turn out onto a serving plate with a rim.

Meanwhile, combine the three milks in a jug, then slowly pour milk mixture over the cake, allowing it to soak in.

Serve slices of cake topped with a dollop of whipped cream and seasonal berries. **Serves 6**

* Golden caster sugar is available from gourmet food shops and selected greengrocers; substitute caster sugar.

Monkey bun

310g unsalted butter

3⅓ cups (500g) plain flour

1¼ tbs dried instant yeast

1 tbs caster sugar

1 tbs finely grated
   orange zest

1 tsp ground cinnamon

¾ cup (180ml) warm milk

2 eggs, lightly beaten

⅔ cup firmly packed
   (200g) brown sugar

1 tbs golden syrup

12 pitted cherries, or other
   seasonal berries, or small
   pieces of dark chocolate

Melt 60g butter in a small saucepan over low heat, then cool.

Combine flour, yeast, caster sugar, zest, cinnamon and 1 tsp sea salt in a bowl. Make a well in the centre, then add melted butter, milk and eggs, and stir well to combine. Place in an oiled bowl, cover with a clean tea towel and set aside in a warm place to prove for 1½ hours or until doubled in size.

Place remaining 250g butter, sugar and golden syrup in a pan over low heat, stirring until melted and combined.

Grease a 2.5L kugelhopf pan. Knock down dough, turn out onto a lightly floured surface and knead for 3–4 minutes until smooth and elastic. Divide dough into 12 portions and form into balls. Push a cherry into the centre of each, pinching dough to encase the fruit completely. Dip each dough ball into syrup, turning until well coated, then layer in the prepared pan, pouring over any remaining syrup. Cover with a clean tea towel and set aside to prove in a warm place for a further 1 hour or until the dough has risen to reach the top of the mould.

Preheat the oven to 190°C. Place pan on a baking tray (some sauce may bubble over during baking). Bake for 10 minutes, then reduce to 160°C and bake for a further 20–25 minutes. Stand in the pan for 5 minutes before carefully turning out onto a plate to serve.

Serves 6–8

Almond croissant pudding with creme anglaise and raspberries

4 almond croissants
   (preferably day-old), torn
   into large chunks
4 eggs
½ cup (110g) caster sugar
300ml milk
300ml pure (thin) cream
1 vanilla bean, split, seeds
   scraped
Finely grated zest of
   ½ orange
2 tbs brandy
Toasted flaked almonds, fresh
   raspberries and creme
   anglaise* or cream,
   to serve
Icing sugar, to dust

Grease the base and sides of a 1-litre terrine or loaf pan and line with baking paper. Pack croissants into the terrine or pan. Set aside.

Whisk the eggs and sugar in a large bowl until just combined.

Place the milk, cream and vanilla pod and seeds in a saucepan over low heat and bring to just below boiling point, then gradually pour the warm milk mixture into the egg mixture, whisking constantly. Add the orange zest and brandy and whisk well to combine. Pour over the croissants in the pan and set aside at room temperature for 1 hour so the custard soaks in – this will make for a much lighter pudding.

Preheat the oven to 180°C. Bake the pudding for 45 minutes until just set and golden on top (cover with foil if it's browning too quickly).

Allow to cool slightly, then turn out and slice. Scatter with almonds and raspberries, drizzle with creme anglaise or cream and serve dusted with icing sugar. **Serves 6–8**

* Creme anglaise is available from gourmet food shops.

Sticky toffee ginger pudding

1 x 500g store-bought ginger
   cake, cut into 12 slices
Vanilla ice cream, to serve
½ cup stem ginger in syrup*,
   chopped

Caramel sauce*
2½ cups (330g) caster sugar
½ cup (125ml) water
300ml thickened cream

Preheat the oven to 170°C.

Wrap cake slices together in foil and place in the oven for 10 minutes or until warm.

For the caramel sauce, combine sugar and water in a saucepan over low heat, stirring until sugar dissolves.

Increase heat to medium and cook, without stirring, occasionally brushing down the sides of the pan with a damp pastry brush, for 8–10 minutes until a golden caramel forms.

Remove from heat, then immediately pour in cream (be careful, as mixture will bubble, then seize).

Return pan to stove over a low heat and cook, stirring, for 1–2 minutes until smooth.

To serve, layer 3 slices of the warmed cake on each of 4 plates with tablespoonfuls of vanilla ice cream, drizzle over 1 cup caramel sauce and top with chopped stem ginger. **Serves 4**

* Stem ginger in syrup is available in jars from selected supermarkets and delis; substitute glace ginger. Store caramel sauce in an airtight container in the fridge for up to 2 weeks; makes 2 cups.

Rhubarb & strawberry crumbles

1 bunch rhubarb, trimmed,
  cut into 3cm lengths
¼ cup (55g) caster sugar
2 tsp finely grated orange
  zest, plus ½ cup (125ml)
  orange juice
2 tsp cornflour
250g punnet strawberries,
  hulled, quartered
Pure (thin) cream, to serve

Crumble topping

100g unsalted butter
½ cup (110g) caster sugar
⅔ cup (100g) plain flour,
  sifted
⅔ cup (100g) pistachio
  kernels

Preheat the oven to 180°C. Line a baking tray with baking paper.

For the crumble topping, place the butter, sugar, flour and pistachios in a food processor and pulse until mixture resembles coarse crumbs. Spread onto the lined tray and refrigerate while you make the filling.

Place the rhubarb, sugar and orange zest and juice in a saucepan over medium-low heat. Cook, stirring, for 5 minutes or until just tender. Combine the cornflour with 1 tablespoon cold water, stirring to dissolve, then add to the pan. Cook, stirring, for 1–2 minutes until slightly thickened, then stir in the strawberries.

Divide the rhubarb mixture among 6 x 1-cup (250ml) cleaned cans or ramekin dishes. Sprinkle over the crumble topping, then bake for 20 minutes or until topping is golden and the strawberries have released all their juices.

Drizzle the crumbles with cream and serve. **Makes 6**

tutti frutti puddings

185g unsalted butter,
 softened
¾ cup (165g) caster sugar
2 eggs
2 tsp finely grated lemon zest
1½ cups (225g) self-raising
 flour
½ cup (125ml) milk
Custard, or pure (thin) cream,
 to serve

Toppings
Lemon curd*
Strawberry jam
Blackcurrant jam
Orange marmalade
Ginger marmalade with
 chopped stem ginger
Orange conserve
Fig jam with sliced fresh figs

Preheat the oven to 170°C.

Grease and line the bases and sides of 6 x 1-cup (250ml) dariole moulds. Place ½ tablespoon of your preferred topping in each.

Using electric beaters, beat butter and sugar until thick and pale. Add eggs 1 at a time, beating well after each addition. Fold in lemon zest. Sift over flour and fold in until combined, then stir through the milk until mixture is a soft dropping consistency.

Divide batter among moulds, filling to 1cm from rim to allow for rising. Cover each mould first with a piece of pleated baking paper, then a piece of pleated foil and secure with kitchen string.

Place moulds in a roasting pan and pour in enough boiling water to come halfway up sides. Bake for 40–45 minutes until a skewer inserted into the centre of the puddings comes out clean. Remove ramekins from pan and set aside to rest for 5 minutes.

Turn out puddings onto a platter and top each with another ½ tablespoon of topping. Serve with custard or cream. **Serves 6**

* Lemon curd is available from delis and gourmet food shops.

Index

ABC
Books

The ABC 'Wave' device is a trademark of the
Australian Broadcasting Corporation and is used
under licence by HarperCollins*Publishers* Australia.
The *delicious.* trademark is used under licence from the
Australian Broadcasting Corporation and NewsLifeMedia.

delicious. Bake comprises recipes and photographs originally published in *delicious. Faking It* (2008),
delicious. Quick Smart Cook (2009), *delicious. More Please* (2010), *delicious. Simply the Best* (2011),
delicious. Home Cooking (2012) and *delicious. Love to Cook* (2013)

First published in Australia in 2015
by HarperCollins*Publishers* Australia Pty Limited
ABN 36 009 913 517
harpercollins.com.au

HarperCollins*Publishers*
Level 13, 201 Elizabeth Street, Sydney NSW 2000, Australia
Unit D1, 63 Apollo Drive, Rosedale Auckland 0632, New Zealand
A 53, Sector 57, Noida, UP, India
1 London Bridge Street, London, SE1 9GF, United Kingdom
2 Bloor Street East, 20th floor, Toronto, Ontario M4W 1A8, Canada
195 Broadway, New York NY 10007, USA

National Library of Australia Cataloguing-in-Publication entry:
Little, Valli, author.
  Delicious: bake / Valli Little.
  978 0 7333 3365 1 (pbk.)
  Baking.
641.71

Author photo by Damian Bennett
Photography by Brett Stevens, Ian Wallace, Jeremy Simons
Styling by David Morgan, Louise Pickford
Cover and internal design by Hazel Lam, HarperCollins Design Studio
Typesetting by Judi Rowe, Agave Creative Group
Colour reproduction by Graphic Print Group, Adelaide SA
Printed and bound in China by RR Donnelley

5 4 3 2 1   15 16 17 18